Jack-Archie King

Martha A. Anthony ☺

Lucy Ruth

Merry Christmas "2011"
Hunter and Sara

Love you.
Nana

God Creates
and so much more…

Illustrations by: Jill R. Wiebe-King

Authors: Martha A. Anthony and Lucille B. Ruth

Press-On Publishing

www.pressonpublishing.com

pressonpublishing@gmail.com

Scripture quotations marked NLT are taken from the
Holy Bible, New Living Translation, copyright 1996.
Used by permission of Tyndale House Publishers, Inc.,
Wheaton, Illinois 60189. All rights reserved.

Scripture taken from the New King James Version.
Copyright© 1985 by Thomas Nelson Inc.
Used by permission. All rights reserved.

Scripture taken from the HOLY BIBLE, NEW
INTERNATIONAL VERSION®. NIV® Copyright©
1973, 1978, 1984, 1985 by International Bible Society.
Used by permission of Zondervan. All rights reserved.

ISBN # 978-0-9821334-0-8

Cataloging-in-Publication Data is on file with the
Library of Congress.

Press-On Publishing, Inc.*
P.O. Box 3982
Richmond, Virginia 23235-7982
www.pressonpublishing.com
pressonpublishing@gmail.com

*"I press on toward the goal to win the prize for which God has
called me heavenward in Christ Jesus." Philippians 3:14, NIV

ACKNOWLEDGEMENTS

We would like to thank Orv Wiebe, Jill's father, for allowing her to use his hands as models for these illustrations.

A thank you to all those who taught us to love the Word of God.
Our thanks to the next generation of parents who petitioned us to pass on this love for the Truth.

A special thank you to Steven Wiebe-King for his artistic consultation throughout this project, and to Wiley Ruth for his expertise in helping us through the financial process in publishing this book.

Publishing a book requires the expertise of an editor and a graphic designer.
Thank you to Tanya Brockett and Haley Hollenbach for fulfilling these roles.

We also appreciate the marketing skills and enthusiasm of Kim Ruth
who has challenged us to think "outside the box."

Dear Moms and Dads,

Welcome to "God Creates!"

God is the potter and we are the clay, and He has given us the privilege of participating in the molding of our children.

We have used the beautiful story of Genesis 1 as our subject matter and have organized this book into two parts. The first part portrays each act of creation in picture with scripture. We suggest that you begin with the pictures. Explore the beauty, order, imagination and the power of God. Then familiarize yourself with the second part of the book, which lists activities relating to each of the pictures.

God had fun creating the earth and everything in it. Our desire is that you have fun with Him and His works through the pictures and the activities. It is our intention that the activities in this book be done at anytime of the day; in your rising up, at the table, outside, or on outings. Choose the activities that are convenient and applicable to your child. We have included a prayer and a Bible verse at the end of each set of activities so that your child can learn to thank God for His great gift of creation and begin memorizing scripture. We hope this book will help you see and experience the excitement of the miracles of creation in fresh ways.

In the beginning God created the heavens and the earth. Now the earth was formless and empty, darkness was over the surface of the deep… *Genesis 1:1–2 (NIV)*

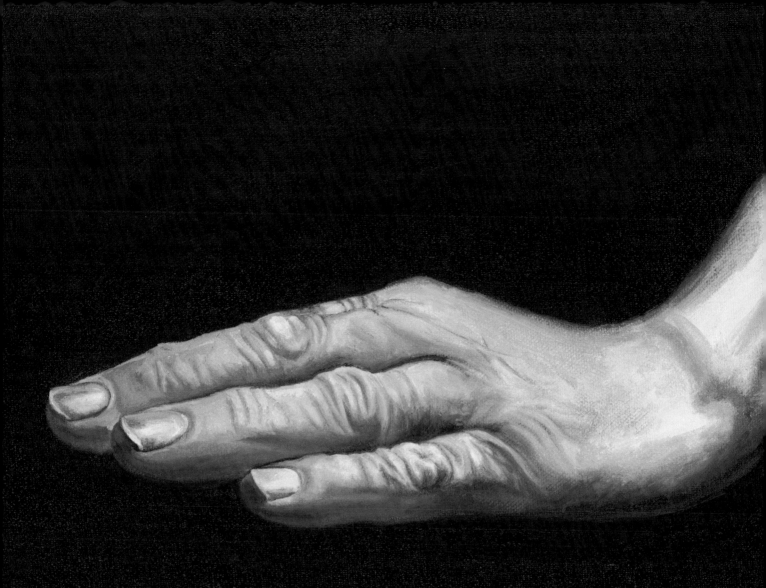

...and the Spirit of God was hovering over the waters. *Genesis 1:2 (NIV)*

And God said, Let there be light: and there was light. *Genesis 1:3 (KJV)*

And God saw the light,
that it was good:…
Genesis 1:4 (KJV)

...and God divided the light from the darkness.

Genesis 1:4 (KJV)

And God called the light Day, and the darkness
he called Night. And the evening and the
morning were the first day. *Genesis 1:5 (KJV)*

And God said, "Let there be space between the waters, to separate water from water." *Genesis 1:6 (NLT)*

And so it was. God made this space to separate the waters above from the waters below. And God called the space "sky." This happened on the second day.

Genesis 1:7–8 (NLT)

And God said, "Let the waters beneath the sky be gathered into one place so dry ground may appear." And so it was. God named the dry ground "land" and the water "seas"…

Genesis 1:9–10 (NLT)

...And God saw that it was good. *Genesis 1:10*
(NLT)

Then God said, "Let the land burst forth with every sort of grass and seed-bearing plant. And let there be trees that grow seed-bearing fruit. The seeds will then produce the kinds of plants and trees from which they came." And so it was. *Genesis 1:11 (NLT)*

The land was filled with seed-bearing plants and trees, and their seeds produced plants and trees of like kind… *Genesis 1:12 (NLT)*

…And God saw that it was good.
This all happened on the third day.
Genesis 1:12–13 (NLT)

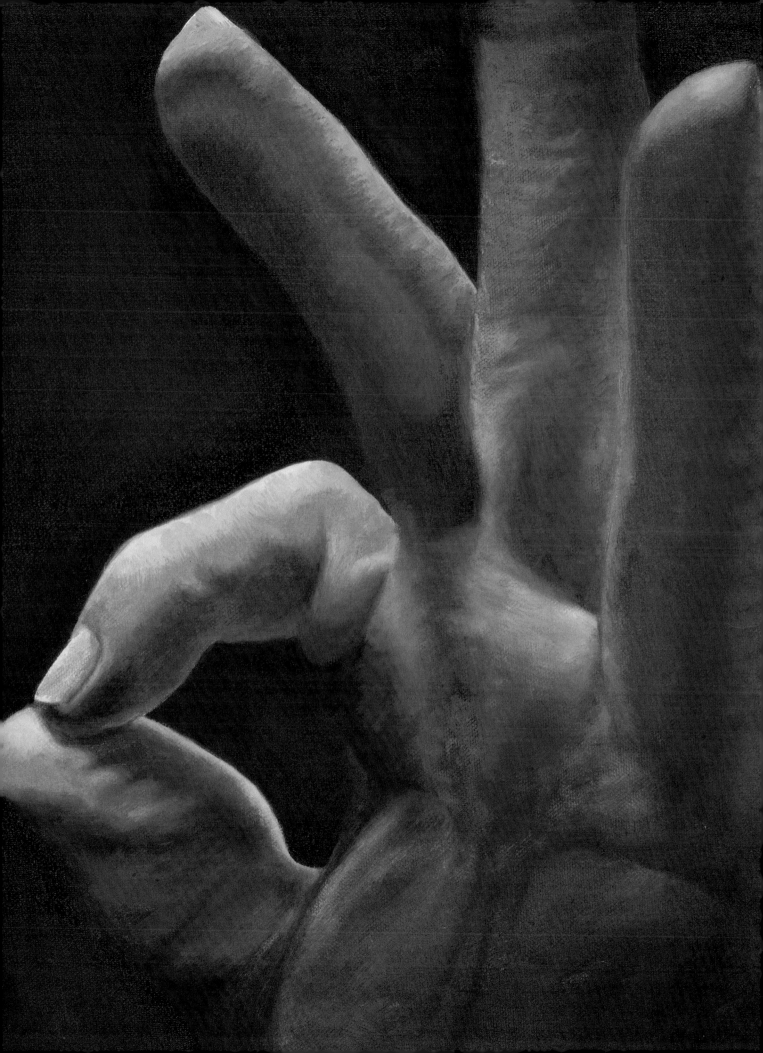

And God said, "Let bright lights appear in the sky to separate the day from the night. They will be signs to mark off the seasons, the days, and the years. Let their light shine down upon the earth." And so it was. For God made two great lights, the sun and the moon, to shine down upon the earth. The greater one, the sun, presides during the day; the lesser one, the moon, presides through the night... *Genesis 1:14–16 (NLT)*

…He also made the stars. God set these lights in the heavens to light the earth, to govern the day and the night, and to separate the light from the darkness… *Genesis 1:16–18 (NLT)*

…And God saw that it was good. This all happened on the fourth day. *Genesis 1:18–19 (NLT)*

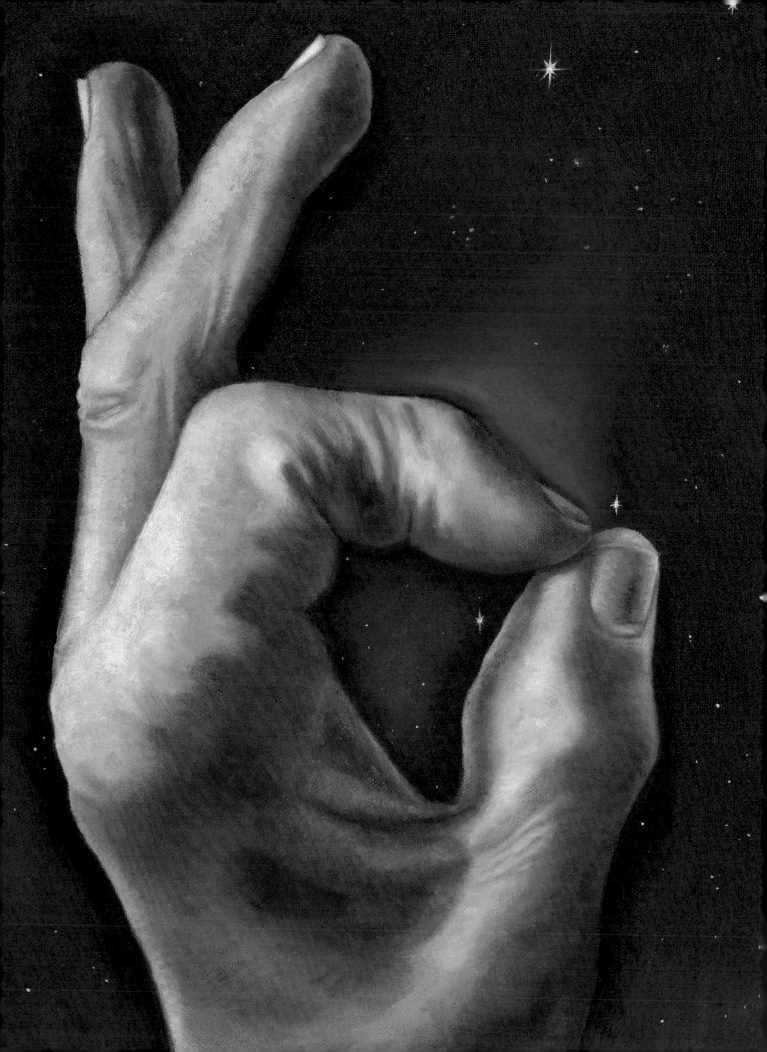

And God said, "Let the waters swarm with fish and other life…" So God created great sea creatures and every sort of fish… Then God blessed them, saying, "Let the fish multiply and fill the oceans…" *Genesis 1:20–22 (NLT)*

And God said, "…Let the skies be filled with birds of every kind." *Genesis 1:20 (NLT)*

…And God saw that it was good. Then God blessed them saying, "…Let the birds increase and fill the earth." This all happened on the fifth day.

Genesis 1:21-23 (NLT)

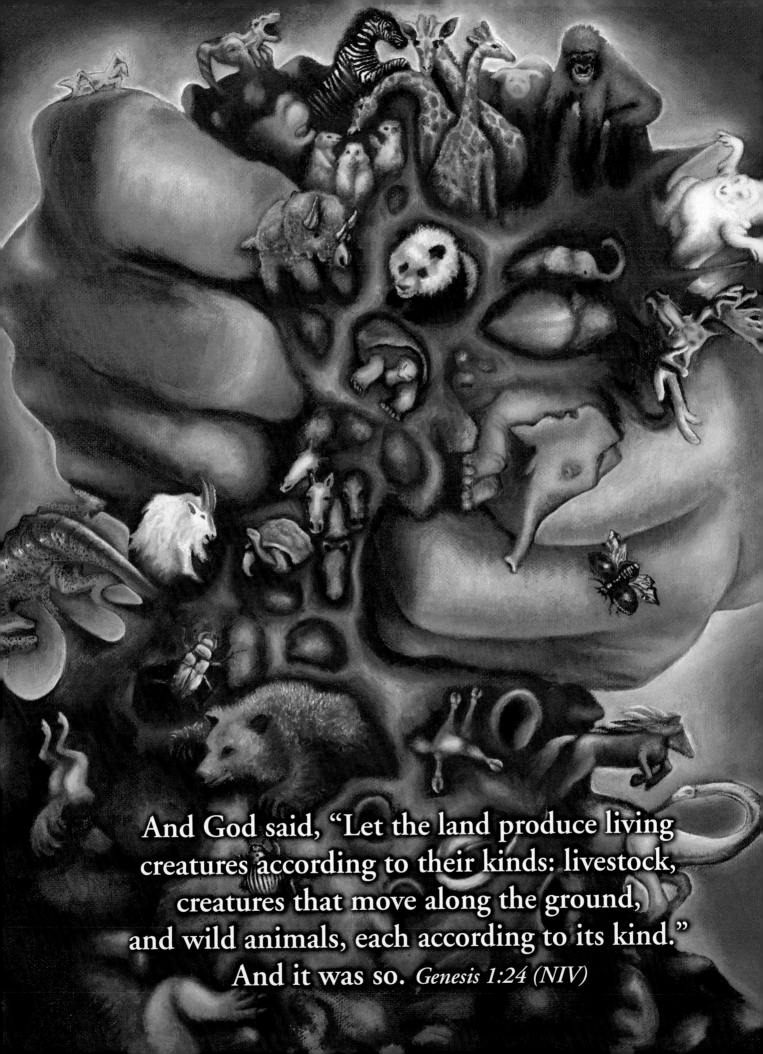

And God said, "Let the land produce living creatures according to their kinds: livestock, creatures that move along the ground, and wild animals, each according to its kind." And it was so. *Genesis 1:24 (NIV)*

God made the wild animals according to their
kinds… and all the creatures that move along
the ground according to their kinds…
Genesis 1:25 (NIV)

...And God saw that it was good.
Genesis 1:25 (NIV)

Then God said, "Let us make man in our image, in our likeness, and let them rule over the fish of the sea and the birds of the air, over the livestock, over all the earth, and over all the creatures that move along the ground."

Genesis 1:26 (NIV)

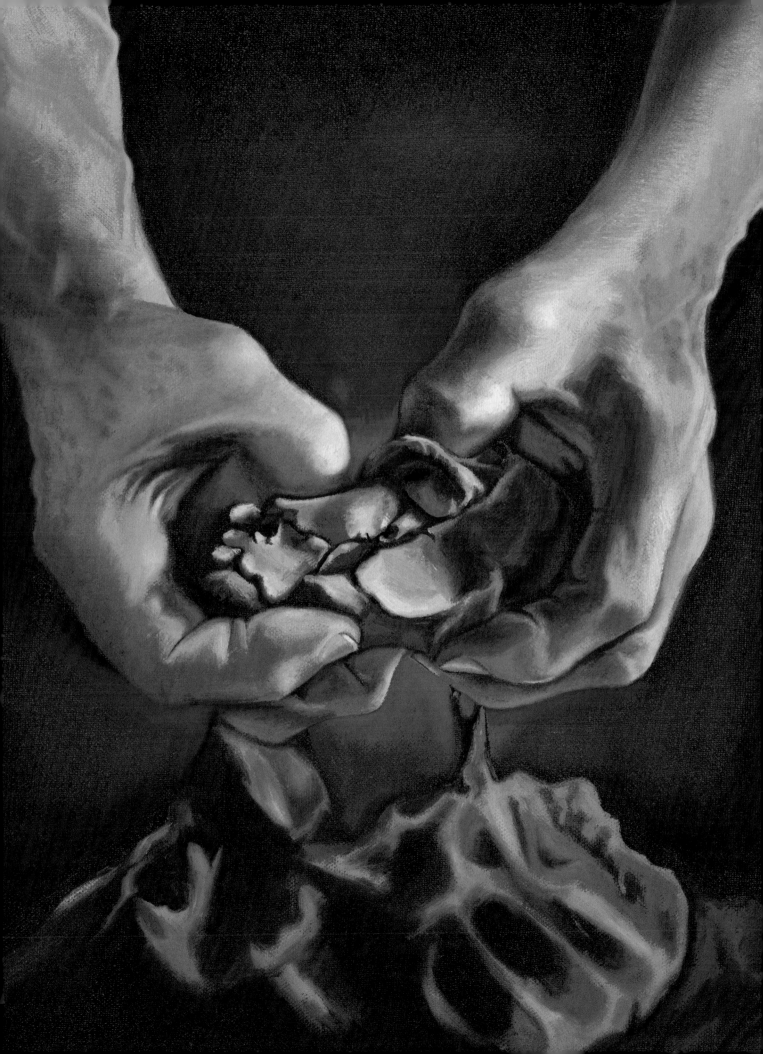

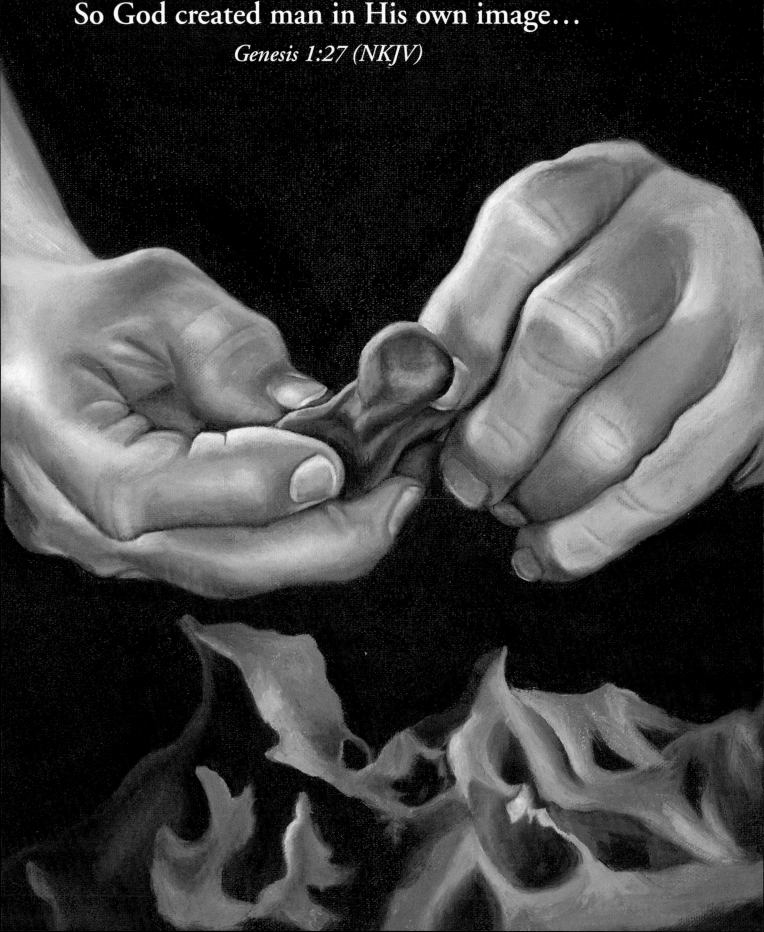

So God created man in His own image…

Genesis 1:27 (NKJV)

...in the image of God He created him;

Genesis 1:27 (NKJV)

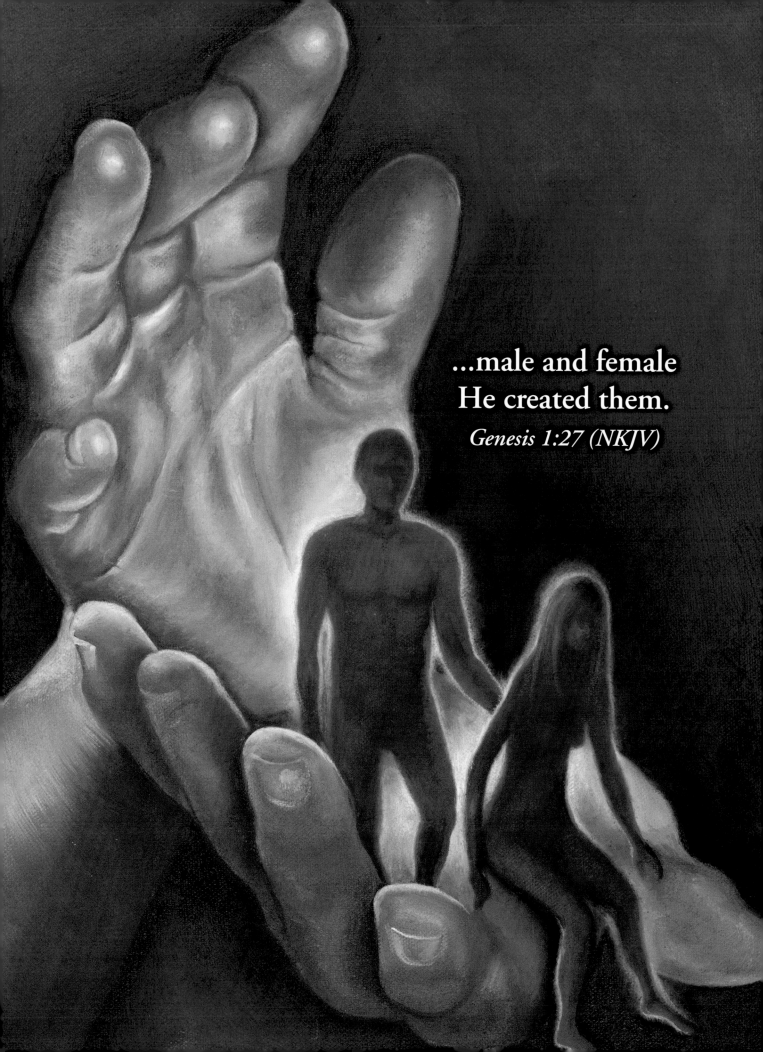

...male and female
He created them.
Genesis 1:27 (NKJV)

God blessed them and said to them,
"Be fruitful and increase in number;
fill the earth and subdue it. Rule over
the fish of the sea and the birds of
the air and over every living creature
that moves on the ground."
Genesis 1:28 (NIV)

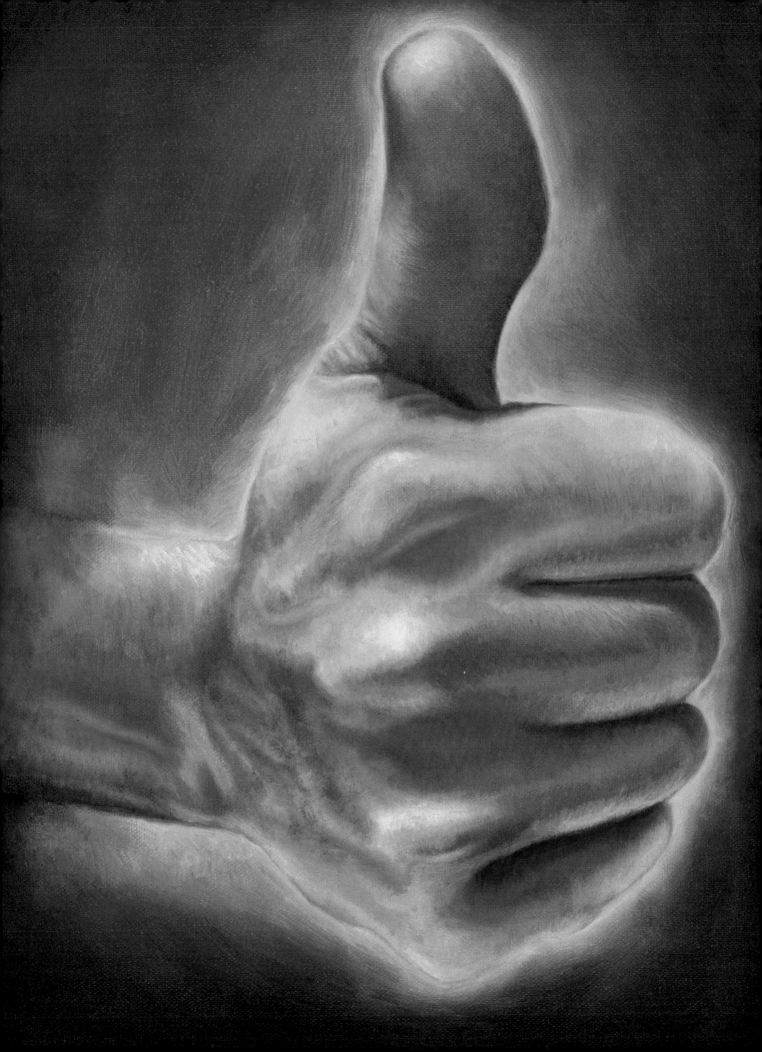

Then God saw everything that He had made, and indeed it was very good. So the evening and the morning were the sixth day. Thus the heavens and the earth, and all the hosts of them, were finished. *Genesis 1:31–2:1 (NKJV)*

By the seventh day God had finished the work that he had been doing; so on the seventh day he rested from all his work. And God blessed the seventh day and made it holy, because on it he rested from all the work of creating that he had done. *Genesis 2:2–3 (NIV)*

Activity and Devotional Guide

Statement 1

The Bible says that it was dark; the earth had no shape; and the Spirit of God was hovering over it.

Ask

"Where in the house can we go where there will be no light?" (Examples: bathroom, closet, cabinet, basement)

Activities

Explain to your child that you are going on an adventure. It will not be scary. Take your child to the places that he or she named and see if it is totally dark. If it is not, continue until you find a place that is totally dark. Then sit down.

1. **STATEMENT:** The Bible says that it was dark.

   QUESTION: Can you see anything in the dark? Why?

   RESTATE: This is what the Bible says it was like—all darkness, all black, and you could not see anything.

2. **STATEMENT:** The earth had no shape. There were no mountains, no trees, and no oceans because the Bible says that the earth had no shape.

   QUESTION: Were there mountains? Were there trees? Were there oceans?

   QUESTION: Can you name something that was missing?

3. **STATEMENT:** The Spirit of God was hovering over the darkness.

GAME: Have your child sit down. While you stand behind the child, play the game **Is My Hand Over Your Head?** Have your child guess if your hand is over his or her head. Tell your child if the guess is correct. (Roles can be reversed.)

RESTATE: As my hand was above your head, so was God above what He was going to create. The Bible says that this was God's position.

Prayer

Thank you, God, that you chose to create the world. Amen.

Psalm 24:1 says, "The earth is the Lord's and the fullness thereof." (NKJV)

Statement 2

"Let there be light."

Activities

Several activities are listed below that could demonstrate light being separated from the darkness. Let your child try one or more of these activities. As they do activities 1–4, have them say, "Let there be light."

1. Walk into a darkened room and turn on a light or flip the light switch.

2. Move into a darkened room and turn on a flashlight.

3. Go outside at night and have your child turn on the headlights of your car.

4. Venture outside and see how dark it is. Then have your child turn on the outside lights.

5. Take a sheet of black paper and a sheet of white paper. Cut the black sheet in half and glue it on half of the white sheet. Explain that this activity reminds us how God divided light and dark.

6. Put a white sock beside a black one and have your child move them farther apart to show separation of light and dark.

7. Using a toilet paper roll, put a dark piece of cloth in one end and a white cloth in the other end. You hold the roll in the middle and have the child grab the cloth from each end of the roll and pull it out to show the separation of light and dark.

8. What symbol or saying does your family use to show that something is good? If you don't have one, make one up and use it every time that God says, "It is good." (In this case, God called the light and the dark good.)

(continued on next page)

Statement 2 continued

Ask

1. Which do you like best—daytime or nighttime? Morning or evening? Why?

2. Is there anything that you do not like about daytime?

3. Is there anything that you do not like about nighttime?

4. What do you like about the light?

5. What do you like about the dark? (If your child says that he doesn't like the dark, remind him that God created light and dark.)

[If appropriate, restate that God's hand hovers over us day and night.]

Prayer

Thank you, God, for day and night, and the light and the dark. Amen.

Psalm 139:12 says, "The darkness and the light are both alike to You." (NKJV) Explain to your child that God sees in the dark as well as in the light.

Statement 3

God separated the waters from the waters with a space called sky.

Activities

1. Have your child place his/her hand in a clear bowl of water. Explain that his/her hand is like the space (sky) with water above it and below it. (Scripture is referring to the space above our atmosphere.)

2. Draw a picture with space (sky) in the center and water above it and below it.

3. If you have blocks, choose one color for the water above and the water below and one color for the space (sky). Have your child build 3 rows of blocks to illustrate the water above, the sky, and the water below.

Prayer

Thank you for creating a space called sky. Amen.

Psalm 19:1 says, "The heavens declare the glory of God and the firmament shows His handiwork." (NKJV)

Statement 4

The world has water and land.

Activity

Show your child a globe or map and look at the difference between the water and the land.

Ask

Ask your child questions like the following:

1. Is there more water or land?
2. When are you in the water?
3. When are you on the land?
4. When are you in the space (sky)?
5. Have your child give the family sign and/or saying for "It is good!"

Prayer

Thank you for creating the water and the land. Amen.

Psalm 104:6–7 says, "The waters stood above the mountains. At your rebuke, they fled." (NKJV)

Statement 5

God created vegetation (trees, flowers, grass, fruits, and vegetables).

Activities/Ask

1. Go outside and find things that God created (twigs, leaves, grass, flowers, etc.).
2. Walk outside and look for seeds (acorns, pine cones, etc.). Start a family collection bowl. This will build sensitivity for God's creation.
3. Show your child different kinds of seeds and look at the different sizes.
4. Give your child seeds to plant and watch them grow. (You can use a plastic cup with soil or a wet paper towel so that you can open it and they can watch the seed grow. Radish seeds or bean seeds work well. You can also try alfalfa sprouts.)
5. Find some edible seeds and let your child eat the seeds. (Examples: sunflower seeds, pumpkin seeds, popcorn, and nuts.)
6. Ask the child to name a fruit or vegetable. Discuss that some come from seeds and that some come from roots (carrots, potatoes).

(continued on next page)

Statement 5 continued

7. Prepare a plate with different fruits and vegetables. Have the child name the food. If the food has a seed, have him/her show you the seed(s) and remove the seed(s).

8. Take a bag and place a food that contains seeds in it. Let them try to guess what is in the bag by feeling the outside of the bag.

9. Have them name their favorite fruit or vegetable. Cut it and see if it has seeds. Then let them eat it.

10. Find one or two edible plants that are seeds (wild rice, asparagus, alfalfa, prickly pear, strawberries, blueberries, etc.).

11. Let your child help plant flowers, shrubs, etc. Encourage them to get their hands in the dirt.

12. Ask your child, if they were a plant, which one would they be and why. You could be a redwood because it is so big that it looks like it reaches the heavens, or you could be a daisy because it represents joy, light, aliveness, and hope.

13. Visit a botanical garden.

14. Have your child give your family sign and/ or saying for "It is good!"

Prayer

PARENT: Thank you, God, for creating so many different kinds of fruits, vegetables, plants and trees. Amen.

CHILD: Thank you, God, for [name their favorite fruit or veggie.] Amen.

Psalm 104:14 says, "He causes grass to grow for the cattle, and vegetation for the service of man…" (NKJV)

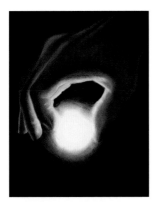

Statement 6

God made the sun, the moon, and the stars.

Ask

1. What light is in the sky in the daytime?

2. What light is in the sky at nighttime?

3. Does the moon always appear round? In what other shapes does the moon appear?

4. Does it ever look like a piece of fruit? Which one?

5. Can you look at the sun?

6. Why can't you?

Activities

1. Draw a large circle for the sun and a smaller one for the moon. Ask your child to make one also, even if he/she has to copy yours.

2. Go outside with a blanket and lie down. Look at the lights. Have your child show you the lights God created.

3. Have a dark sheet and a white sheet and cut outs of the sun, moon, and stars. Have your child glue them on the right sheet.

   You can have an older child draw or cut out these things for themselves or for their younger siblings.

4. Have your child give the family sign and/or saying for "It is good!"

Statement 7

God said these lights would mark off the seasons, the days, and the years.

Ask

1. Does the sun feel warmer in the winter or summer? Why?

2. What do the trees look like when it is cold?

3. What do they look like when it is warm?

4. Why is there a difference in the way the trees appear?

5. When is it light outside? When is it dark outside?

6. How old are you and how old will you be on your next birthday? Have your child mark his/her birthday on a calendar.

Tell your child that it will be one year from this birthday to the next. (The sun and moon will come up and go down over and over again until one year has passed.)

Prayer

Thank you, Lord, for the lights in the sky, the sun, the moon, and the stars. Thank you for the seasons—winter, spring, summer, and fall—for the days, for the years, and for the day and night. Amen.

Psalm 104:19 says, "He appointed the moon for seasons; the sun knows its going down." (NKJV)

Statement 8

God created great sea creatures and every sort of fish.

Activities/Ask

1. Visit a fish tank at a local aquarium, a doctor's office, or a pet store.

2. Watch the fishing channel or a nature channel on TV.

3. If you're at the beach, explore all the different types of sea life.

4. Take your child fishing, crabbing, or shrimping.

5. Make sugar cookies using a fish or other sea animal cookie cutter.

6. Make a collage of sea life from pictures from the Internet or from nature magazines.

7. Look for coloring books, sticker books, or stickers of sea animals.

8. Find picture books or easy books about sea animals to look through or to read from book stores or your local library.

9. Go to a party store and purchase sea animals that can be hung in your child's room.

10. Find puzzles of sea animals to put together.

11. How are you like a fish? How are you different from a fish?

12. In looking at the pictures, which fish would you be? Why?

Prayer

Thank you, God, for the beautiful colors, shapes, and sizes of the sea animals that you have created. Amen.

Psalm 96:11 says, "Let the sea roar, and all its fullness." (NKJV)

Statement 9

God made every kind of bird.

Activities/Ask

1. Hang a simple bird feeder in a place where you and your child can watch the birds eat. Let your child help to fill it.

2. Make your own bird feeder. Take a pine cone and attach a string to it. Cover the pine cone in peanut butter and roll it in birdseed. Hang it from a tree or from your house.

3. Locate a CD or audio tape of different bird sounds and listen to it. Rejoice over the differences.

4. Check out Websites for different bird calls.

5. Buy coloring books or sticker books of birds.

6. Get nature magazines and cut out bird pictures or print them from the Internet.

7. Find picture books or easy books about birds to look at or to read.

8. Purchase a bird house and watch the birds.

9. Try to imitate the birds you hear outside your house.

10. Collect bird feathers and touch them to your skin. Use them to make a picture.

11. Would you like to be a bird? If so, which one? For example, maybe you could be a peacock so you could be flashy or tuck in your tail; or you could be an eagle because it's strong, powerful, and soars above everything.

12. How are you like a bird? How are you different?

13. Visit a local park that has nature centers or nature walks.

14. Have your child give the family sign and/or saying for "It is good!"

Prayer

God, we thank you for the many different kinds of birds, for the many different colors we see as they fly, and for the sounds they make as they sing. Amen.

Psalm 104:17 says, "…where the birds make their nest. The stork has her home in the fir trees." (NKJV)

Statement 10

God made animals.

Activities/Ask

1. Visit a zoo and observe all the different kinds of animals.

2. If you have a pet, look at it carefully. Ask your child, "How is the pet like you and how is the pet different from you?"

3. Get coloring books or sticker books of animals.

4. Draw animals.

5. Visit a farm.

6. Play with animal toys. (For example, have your child gather all his/her stuffed animals to create a farm, zoo, or jungle scene.)

7. Make an animal out of clay or playdough. (Recipe for playdough on page 68.)

8. Imitate the different sounds that animals make.

9. Read animal stories.

10. Get stickers of animals.

11. Find pictures of animals in magazines or from the Internet and cut them out.

12. Using the pictures your child cut out or the animal toys he/she has played with, have your child create a story.

13. Name a bug. If you were that bug, what could you do that you cannot do now?

14. Have your child give the family sign and/or saying for "It is good!"

Prayer

God, we thank you for all your animals—friendly and unfriendly. We thank you that you made each one so different, and that each animal has a purpose. Amen.

Psalm 8:6–7 says, "You have put all things under his feet… even the beast of the field." (NKJV)

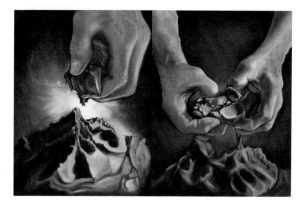

Statement 11

God made man in His image, in His likeness.

Activities/Ask

1. Have your child pick up dirt and sift it through his/her hands.

2. Have your child describe what pieces of things are seen in the dirt.

3. Ask your child how he/she thinks God took the dirt and made people.

4. What is the difference between clay and dirt?

5. Why is it easier to work with clay than dirt?

6. Since God created everything, name some animals He created. How are we different from the animals you named?

7. Name something else that God created. How are we alike or different from what you named?

8. Draw a picture of yourself. Do you look like God?

9. How do you think we are like God?*

10. Design a "created by God" sticker. Put it on yourself and others.

Prayer

Dear God, thank you that you created us in your image. Amen.

Psalm 8:5 says, "For you have made him a little lower than the angels, and you have crowned him with glory and honor." (NKJV)

*Explain that God is three persons—Father, Son, and Holy Spirit. We were created with a spirit, soul, and body. Even with matter, God created in threes—solid, liquid, and gas. [For example, water (liquid), ice (solid), steam (gas).]

Statement 12

God created man in His own image, male and female.

Activities/Ask

1. Have your child create a person using clay or playdough. (See recipe below.)

2. Mix dirt and water to make thick mud. Have your child create a person from the mud.

3. A boy is a male. What are some things boys like to do?

4. Name the males in your family or males you know.

5. Since your dad is a male, what are some things he likes to do?

6. A girl is a female. What are some things girls like to do?

7. Name the females in your family or ones you know.

8. Since your mom is a female, what are some things she likes to do?

9. Why did God create male and female as the beginning of a family?

Prayer

Let the parent thank God for creating them male/female. Encourage your child to thank God for making him or her a boy or a girl. Amen.

Psalm 139:14 says, "I will praise you for I am fearfully and wonderfully made." (NKJV)

Recipe for playdough
2 c flour
2 T cream of tartar
1 ½ c water
½ c salt
1 T oil
Can add food coloring, spices (like cinnamon), or extracts

Mix the first two ingredients together in a bowl. Next, heat the water, salt, and oil to boiling. Stir liquids into dry ingredients. Knead until smooth. Store in airtight container.

Statement 13

God blessed them and He said have babies to fill the earth.

Activities/Ask

1. What makes up a family?
2. Who is in your family?
3. Name some ways God has blessed you and your family.
4. Draw your family.
5. Design a family tree to show how the family has multiplied.
6. What does it mean to be fruitful?
7. Name some ways a person is fruitful.
8. What are some ways we are to rule (take care of) the earth?

Prayer

Dear God, thank you for creating the family. Help us rule over the earth. Amen.

Psalm 133:1 says, "How good and how pleasant it is for brethren to dwell together in unity." (NKJV)

Statement 14

God saw that everything He made was very good.

Activities/Ask

1. Name something difficult that you have learned to do. (Your child could say anything from tying a shoe to juggling a soccer ball.)
2. How did you feel when you finished this?
3. What did God see that He had finished?
4. What did God say when He was finished?
5. Did He change the sign He used?
6. Can you think of another sign that you could use that would express "It is very good!"?

Prayer

Thank you, God, that you work and created us to work. Thank you, God, that you finish what you start, and we can finish what we start. Amen.

Psalm 103:22, says "Bless the LORD, all His works, In all places of His dominion. Bless the LORD, O my soul!" (NKJV)

Statement 15

God rested after finishing His work.

Activities/Ask

1. Show how you rest.

2. How do you feel when you are tired?

3. What happens when your mom, dad, brother, or sister haven't rested?

4. Why does God want us to rest?

5. What are some things that you do when you are tired?

6. What other things rest? (for example: animals)

7. Do they rest the same way that you do?

8. Show how your pet rests.

Prayer

Thank you for showing us that it is a blessing to work and play, but it is also a blessing to rest. Amen.

Psalm 37:37 says, "Rest in the Lord and wait patiently for Him." (NKJV)

Conclusion

SONG

He's Got the Whole World in His Hands

He's got the whole world in His hands,
He's got the whole world in His hands.
He's got the whole world in His hands,
He's got the whole world in His hands.

He's got you and me brother in His hands…
He's got you and me sister in His hands…

(You can make up verses such as mommy
and daddy, grandma and grandpa, aunts
and uncles, friends and pets, etc.)

Other Related Scriptures

Psalm 100:3
Psalm 145:4
Psalm 148
1 Timothy 4:4
Psalm 19:1–4
Psalm 150
Psalm 24:1–2
Psalm 119:73
Nehemiah 9:6
Psalm 136:1–9
Jeremiah 32:17
Psalm 147:7–9

Prayer

(Begin prayer by having your child thank God
for something.) Then pray…

Thank you, Lord, for having the whole world
in your hands. Thank you that you have
[child's name] in your hands. Thank you for
all that you have created. Amen.

Martha Anthony has been an educator for over 30 years. She taught both elementary and middle school. Her delight was working with students of all backgrounds and nationalities. Since retiring, she has enjoyed spending more time with her extended family and with friends. She is passionate about the Word of God and the Lord. She loves to write and travel.

Jill Wiebe-King is a painter and singer-songwriter. She and her husband, Steven, and their two children, Juliet and RobertThomas, live in Richmond, VA. Jill has been painting for 23 years. She has taught art in many settings to children and adults. She is currently writing and performing songs with her husband.

Lucille Ruth has been married to her husband, Wiley, for 44 years. She is the mother of four married children, and the grandmother of nine. While she is an active musician, her passions are her family and bringing "the power of the Word" to both old and young.

*Visit us on our website at **www.pressonpublishing.com** or email us at pressonpublishing@gmail.com.*